BRITAIN'S HERITAGE

Churchyards

Roger Bowdler

AMBERLEY

Acknowledgements

I would like to thank Paul Stamper, Elizabeth Blood, Maddy Gray, David O'Driscoll and C. B. Newham for help with photographs. Sally Strachey and Trevor Proudfoot have helped on issues of stone conservation, and my editor Nick Wright has been helpful throughout. Julian Litten, James Stevens Curl, Tim Knox, and Nicholas Penny have all encouraged me in the pursuit of sepulchral studies, as has my family: Christina, Basil and Iris have been subjected to a lot of grave-digging from the word go. I am only sorry that my mother is no longer alive to read this. I dedicate the book to the memory of Frederick Burgess (1911–66), the greatest historian of churchyard memorials, whose pioneering achievement deserves the greatest respect.

First published 2019

Amberley Publishing
The Hill, Stroud
Gloucestershire, GL5 4EP

www.amberley-books.com

Copyright © Roger Bowdler, 2019

The right of Roger Bowdler to be identified as the Author of this work has been asserted in accordance with the Copyrights, Designs and Patents Act 1988.

ISBN 978 1 4456 9111 4 (paperback)
ISBN 978 1 4456 9112 1 (ebook)

British Library Cataloguing in Publication Data.
A catalogue record for this book is available from the British Library.

Typesetting by Aura Technology and Software Services, India. Printed in the UK.

Contents

1

Introduction

Let's talk of graves, and worms, and epitaphs

William Shakespeare, *Richard II* (*c.* 1595)

Churchyards are not gloomy. They are wonderful spaces, full of history, nature and art; the dead live on in spirit and through their memorials. Churchyards form the setting for Britain's places of worship, and are of the first order of importance for that reason alone. Their significance is deeper than their visual allure: they are the resting place of generation after generation of our forebears. Some churchyards have been in use for over a thousand years: there can be forty generations or more lying at rest in God's Acre, and in places, even more. Britain has a rich and unsurpassed inheritance of outdoor monuments erected over these graves.

This short book will try to point out some of the reasons why these places matter so much, and to everybody. Social history and geology; religious belief and the rise of literacy; lettering and the history of taste; carving and poetry; and the attempts of the British to accept the inevitability of death and to come to terms with sorrow: these are some of the topics touched upon in a visit to the tombs.

What is a churchyard? It is an enclosed space around a place of worship, devoted to burial and administered by the parish. The term is virtually synonymous with graveyard. A burial ground tends not to contain a church: it might surround a chapel, or it might be a stand-alone enclosure for depositing the dead, opened as an overflow when the churchyard became too full. The term cemetery (from the Greek word *koimeterion*, or place of rest) tends to have classical overtones, and refers to a detached place of burial often outside the town walls; it was used for the new wave of landscaped places of burial which started to be opened

Monument to Richard and Elizabeth Norris (d. 1779) at St Mary at Finchley (London Borough of Barnet). This unusual memorial includes outdoor sculpture of a grieving woman, perhaps based on the classical tale of Agrippina mourning over the ashes of her husband Germanicus. Tombs can possess great emotional resonance, even hundreds of years on.

St Mary's church, Singleton (Sussex). The setting of this eleventh-century church is greatly enhanced by the presence of tombs all around. Forty generations or more of parishioners may be buried here, giving the churchyard deep meaning to present and future communities. (Postcard of 1907)

from the 1820s onwards, and which are not covered here. This book is about churchyards (in Scotland, the kirkyard), and particularly the memorials erected in them, but it will alight on some other sorts of burial ground too.

There are 10,000 churchyards in England alone, and some contain hundreds of historic memorials. The sheer quantity of our sepulchral heritage is daunting, and this has discouraged most from undertaking any survey on a national scale. Churchyards are local in their very essence: they are the resting places of individuals who made up communities, and their inscriptions contain remarkable messages

The tombstone of Thomas Thetcher at Winchester Cathedral (Hampshire). This soldier died in 1764 after 'drinking small beer when hot'. It has now been renewed three times, to preserve this remarkable inscription; monuments are appeals to memory, so when their legibility is lost, so is much of their value. (Postcard of 1908)

from the past which can still be heard today. This book can only paint the story of graveyards in the broadest terms, and select just at a few memorials. If it awakens curiosity and the desire to explore the thousands of others out there, then it has succeeded in its mission.

Did you know?

Thomas Thetcher was a soldier who died in 1764. His tombstone outside Winchester Cathedral has been replaced twice, to reserve its remarkable inscription about his death from drinking 'small beer'. An American soldier, Bill Wilson, saw this in 1918 and kept it in mind: he went on to found Alcoholics Anonymous.

Masons and architects produced remarkable and enduring memorials to the dead: regional differences based on the availability of stone, and on custom and taste, determined what these would look like. Relishing this variety is one of the great pleasures of exploring graveyards. From the seventeenth century, a wider social range of persons was starting to be remembered with memorials. Rising literacy, rising prosperity and a growing desire for remembrance lay beneath this social phenomenon. Religious belief affected their messages, and developments in design changed their appearance. The story of the British tombstone is a complicated one, with many discoveries and connections to be made.

Tombstones shed light on many aspects of the past. Scipio Africanus was eighteen years old when he died, a slave who became a nobleman's page. His head and footstones at Henbury (Bristol) have been renewed, and tell a double story of barbarous treatment and posthumous affection.

The rise in family history and a growing relish for understanding the places we live in each offer hope that the churchyard will be seen as relevant and important to a modern audience. Great advances have been made recently in the sympathetic management of the precious ecology of churchyards. When it comes to the upkeep of man-made heritage, the story is less positive. There are already a number of books about the natural aspects of churchyards: in this book it is very much the man-made elements which are centre-stage.

Many monuments are in steady decline: inscriptions are weathering away, and frequently the larger tombs are collapsing. Caring for the church is daunting enough for a parish. Aren't tombs the responsibility of the families who raised them? Shouldn't they be caring for them? And in any case, shouldn't we just let them go? The dead are dead, and their tombs are bound to follow. Aren't they the products of yesterday's vanity?

This book sets out to explain why we should cherish our graveyards, and do everything in our power to ward off decay and collapse. Thomas Gray's 'Elegy in a Country Churchyard', published in 1751, took the reader on a journey to a rural graveyard and commended the modest memorials to the rustic dead as a prompt for reflection on life, death, status, opportunity, memory and history (and much else besides). One of the best-loved works in the English language, its verses continue to explain why the British churchyard deserves everyone's attention. And in an age in which everyone's history is increasingly prominent, the places where everyone's forebears lie become of ever wider interest. No better launch for this book can be offered than some lines from the 'Elegy':

The churchyard of St Mary's, Painswick (Gloucestershire), is renowned as one of Britain's loveliest. The combination of outstanding tombs, from the Cotswold school of masons, and the unsurpassed ninety-nine yew trees make this a pilgrimage site for all admirers of funereal art.

    Beneath those rugged elms, that yew-tree's shade,
    Where heaves the turf in many a mould'ring heap,
    Each in his narrow cell for ever laid,
    The rude forefathers of the hamlet sleep.

    ...The boast of heraldry, the pomp of pow'r,
    And all that beauty, all that wealth e'er gave,
    Awaits alike th' inevitable hour.
    The paths of glory lead but to the grave.

    ...Can storied urn or animated bust
    Back to its mansion call the fleeting breath?
    Can honour's voice provoke the silent dust,
    Or Flatt'ry soothe the dull cold ear of Death?

Perhaps not: but the efforts of the centuries to come to terms with mortality still stand outdoors, all over the British Isles. They aren't dismal at all. Churchyards are some of the most life-affirming places of all.

2
Churchyards: History to 1700

Much of the archaeological record in this land is derived from funerary tributes to the dead. What part does the churchyard play in the story of burial places? The origins of the church-centred graveyards remain unclear, and the story varies from place to place.

The human need to love and be loved, to identify and to remember, has informed memorials for millennia. Monuments to the dead formed the most enduring remains from antiquity, and the imagination can conceive of a link between standing stones and churchyard tombs. It is, however, a tenuous one. In terms of memorials raised to named and recognisable individuals, located in cemeteries on the edge of settlements, the story begins in Roman Britain. Here, a strong outdoor tradition arose. Collections of monuments at Chester, Gloucester, Colchester and elsewhere testify to the timeless desire mourners have to pay tributes to the dead in enduring tombstone form. These were rediscovered from the 1600s, and some early modern tombstones from the post-medieval period echoed Roman memorials in their design.

In post-Roman times, Anglo-Saxon burial increasingly took place in cemeteries. Excavation suggests that these pagan sites were not yet centred around places of worship, and just how the two came together to create the churchyard is a phenomenon still to be fully understood. Honouring the dead is a deep-rooted sentiment, and urging Christian converts to reject their long-established modes of burial, and leave their ancestral burial places behind in favour of new graveyards, must have presented the early Church with one of its greatest challenges. Consecrated churchyards on the Continent were mentioned by Gregory, Bishop of Tours, in the 570s, and a key English date identified by historians is 752, when Cuthbert, Archbishop of Canterbury, obtained Papal permission for churchyards in towns. The eighth century is seen by some as a key time for the emergence of a recognisable English tradition of burial around a church, although in many places the parish church itself did not appear until the eleventh century or even later; in Scotland, many parishes were not formed until the early twelfth century.

Some churchyards have a powerful connection between the present day and the ancient past. Nowhere shows the continuity between ancient worship and Christianity more clearly than the churchyard at Rudston (East Yorkshire), where Britain's tallest standing stone stands immediately beside the church, surrounded by modest tombstones. St Lawrence's church at West Wycombe (Buckinghamshire) stands within an Iron Age hillfort: its magnificent Georgian church and the Dashwood Mausoleum create a rich historical layering. Taplow (Buckinghamshire) has lost its church, but one formerly stood beside the large *hlaew* or burial mound, dated to the seventh century, which has yielded rich grave goods: a practice which was to disappear with conversion to Christianity. Few places show so eloquently the transition from pagan to Christian practices.

The earliest Christian memorials of all were outdoor ones, and crosses are the type which has most often survived to the present day. Our knowledge is literally fragmentary: many weathered memorials were reused in later church rebuildings, as at Bakewell (Derbyshire), where there are hundreds of older carved stones recovered during Victorian reconstruction

The standing stone at Rudston (East Yorkshire) is dramatic evidence of the continuity of ancient pagan sites with churchyards. Britain's tallest monolith, some 25 feet tall, it would have possessed clear symbolic significance to all who saw it. (Postcard of 1913)

work of the late medieval church, and which afford clear evidence of the sort of outdoor tombs which once existed in early churchyards. Anglo-Saxon crosses survive in considerable numbers across England; whether these marked individual or dynastic graves, or were general guardian presences for the graveyard, is unknown but there is no doubting their significance as early survivals of outdoor commemoration. In St Mary's churchyard, Gosforth (Northumberland), a sandstone cross, 4.5 metres high, survives from the early tenth century; even more remarkable is its combination of Christian symbolism with scenes from Norse mythology. Perhaps the most renowned pre-Conquest memorial type is the hogback. Found generally in the Viking-influenced northern areas of England and in central and southern Scotland, but not (curiously) in Scandinavia, these splendid hump-roofed covers can have bears at either end, clutching the block. Penrith, in Cumbria, contains a fine group of memorials from this time, including hogbacks and cross-shafts.

Archaeological excavations of churchyards have advanced understanding of medieval practices. The investigations at Wharram Percy (North Yorkshire) have not only uncovered the remains of the long-dead villagers; reused Roman coffins have been found too, which suggests a conscious attempt to re-appropriate their dignity for burials in the eleventh century. Archaeology has brought forensic analysis to bear on recovered skeletal remains in a number of graveyard excavations, when redevelopment (like the bringing of the Eurostar line to St Pancras Station in London, across a Georgian graveyard) has required the disinterment of the dead. Such disturbance has, on the plus side, greatly added to our understanding of how earlier populations lived and died. Mercifully, in the vast

Above left: Fragments of Anglo-Saxon churchyard monuments at All Saints' church, Bakewell (Derbyshire). These were reused as building materials in the medieval church, and revealed during nineteenth-century restoration. They are the largest English collection of early outdoor memorial fragments to survive. (Elizabeth Blood)

Above right: The Anglo-Saxon cross in Gosforth churchyard (Northumberland), dating from around 950. Over 4 metres tall, this is an exceptional example of a well-established type of outdoor memorial which served as guardians watching over the graveyard. Others would have been made of timber, and have perished. (Wikimedia)

Left: A rare group of pre-Conquest monuments still in the churchyard, at St Andrew's, Penrith (Cumbria). The group is collectively known as the 'Giant's Grave' and has been linked with a tenth-century king of Cumberland.

majority of cases, the dead continue to rest underground in God's Acre. This traditional name for a churchyard derives from the early custom of setting aside an acre of ground around the church for burials. In later medieval times, charnel vaults were created under some churches (most dramatically at Rothwell, Northants) where bones which grave-diggers had unearthed were stored, awaiting their re-assembly at the Day of Judgment.

From the thirteenth century onwards, more evidence survives for outdoor memorials, including mentions of churchyard tombs in people's wills. Medieval outdoor tombs were once thought to have been very rare, but modern scholarship is starting to revise this assumption: the number of English examples identified in the most thorough recent survey has now passed 3,000. Stones would be reused for building material when weathered and unidentifiable, while other markers have sunk below the ground.

A few churches have retained their outdoor grave-markers: Limpley Stoke (Somerset) has an exceptional collection of slabs still outside, marking the graves. Often, formerly outdoor tombs have been brought inside for protection: drainage holes cut into effigial slabs, enabling rain water to run out, are the tell-tale signs that these once had to withstand the elements. Late medieval chest tombs, embellished with traceried flanks and sometimes inscriptions, are quite numerous still and pointed the way to later monuments. Excavation has also indicated the widespread presence of sockets and post-holes, used for the reception of wooden grave-markers. The appearance of these cross-shafts and gabled crosses is known to us through illustrations in religious texts: from illuminated Books of Hours, containing illustrations accompanying the prayers for the dead,

A late medieval chest tomb at Rodney Stoke (Somerset). Modern scholarship is discovering that there are more external monuments from this period than was once thought to be the case.

Death in the medieval churchyard: this fifteenth-century French woodcut shows a variety of tall crosses and gabled wooden memorials of the type which once stood in northern graveyards. From *Le grant kalendrier et compost des Bergiers* (Nicolas le Rouge, Troyes, 1496).

The gravemarker of Ann Green (d. 1518), Alstonefield (Staffordshire); this may well be the earliest identified and dated headstone in England.

and from early printed devotional works. Some headstones bearing early sixteenth-century dates can be found too: at Broadway (Worcestershire) is an arched stone bearing the date 1516, and Alstonefield (Staffordshire) is what is thought to be the oldest named headstone of all, to Ann Green who died in April 1518.

Churchyards today are regarded as tranquil places of rest and contemplation, but this was not always the case. Fairs, plays, markets, archery practice, meetings and even executions have been recorded as having taken place inside them; having relatively clear open space would have facilitated holding these events. They were places of punishment and of ritual humiliation too, as is attested by the survival in numerous places of stocks.

Churchyards were used for other purposes beside burial. These stocks at Ottery St Mary (Devon), probably eighteenth-century, show how graveyards were social spaces as well as religious and commemorative ones. (Postcard of *c.* 1900)

Did you know?

Churchyards could be places of public punishment. Sets of stocks survive in many churchyards. Malefactors would be held captive in them, subject to the parish's ridicule, and surrounded by tombs – reminders of death and judgment to come.

The Reformation of the sixteenth century had profound effects on attitudes to death and the after-life, but the social need to mark the passing of lives, and record the obligations of survivors to the dead, ensured that monuments went on being erected. England has a rich heritage of internal church monuments which survived the religious changes of the sixteenth century. The early modern, post-Reformation British churchyard is even less studied than the medieval one, and a picture of its overall development has yet to emerge. The cross would have been a controversial form of memorial in Protestant England, so disappeared during the Reformation as a tomb type, but chest tombs and other forms of grave-marker continued to appear. Steadily rising levels of wealth, and a growing sense of asserting identity, fuelled the demand for memorials, and rising levels of literacy made the messages of tombs of ever wider relevance. Weathering has eroded many outdoor tombs, and early wooden grave-markers have long since perished. The survival rates are very patchy and the picture is incomplete but it is a generally accepted view that legible tombstones start to be more commonly encountered from the mid-seventeenth century.

The story was very different in Scotland. The Scottish Reformation Parliament of 1560 ordered proposals for Church reform, published as *The Book of Discipline*. This censured intramural burial, or burial inside the church, an interdiction which was strengthened in 1588 by the Church of Scotland's General Assembly. While some indoor burials continued to take place, Scotland was far in advance of the rest of Britain in developing a culture of higher status outdoor monuments. Nowhere is this seen so memorably as in Greyfriars Kirkyard in Edinburgh, opened in 1562 as the city's central burial ground. Lavish outdoor memorials

Greyfriars Kirkyard, Edinburgh. Opened in 1562 in a former monastic enclosure, this became the city's chief burial ground and gave rise to a spectacular array of outdoor memorials, unsurpassed in the British Isles.

were erected from then on, echoing internal church monuments, and forming perhaps the greatest sepulchral ensemble in the British Isles. Elsewhere, new burial forms developed such as the family burial enclosure or lair, and the mausoleum (or large above-ground structure for burials) as a building type can trace its origins to Scotland too.

In the age of the Metaphysical Poets, that flourishing of mid-seventeenth-century religious and philosophical speculation, thinking on death and the life hereafter gave meditations in graveyards a new piquancy. 'A Walke into Church-yards, and Charnels, though it be sad and melancholy, by reason of the dolefull obiects therein obvious, hath yet ne'ertheless something in it agreeable to content good Soules,' wrote Puget de la Serre in *The Mirour which Flatters Not* (1639). Besides attending services and performing private devotions, the devout could also pursue a form of spiritual exercise by studying the tombs of the dead. The social purposes of monuments of remembrance and honour were discussed by John Weever in the earliest book in English devoted to tombs, his *Ancient Funerall Monuments* of 1631. Churchyard memorials were starting to increase in number at this time as more people aspired to leave a posthumous mark behind them: Sir Thomas Browne's *Urne-Buriall* (1658) is perhaps the most enduring work on mortality and remembrance from this intense period of reflecting on death. And rising literacy levels were giving the act of recording names and dates a wider appeal too, which further boosted the appeal of permanent monuments.

New groups were looking for posthumous recognition through monuments, besides the Church of England. One outcome of the upheaval of the Interregnum of the 1650s was the return of a Jewish community to England: their strict religious laws concerning burial necessitated the opening of dedicated burial grounds, the earliest of which opened in 1657; the oldest to survive in its original form is the Alderney Road Jewish Cemetery in Stepney, London, opened in 1697 for the Ashkenazi community. Around the same time, the renowned Bunhill Fields opened just north of the City of London. This was a burial ground for those who did not wish to lie in consecrated ground, and it became a renowned dormitory of Nonconformity. The memorials in each of these burial grounds drew on established traditions of churchyard tombs; other sects, such as the Quakers, opted for deliberately plainer forms of grave-marking in their burial grounds.

Bunhill Fields was opened in 1662 as an unconsecrated, non-Church of England burial ground on the edge of the City of London. It became celebrated as the embodiment of the capital's proud dissenting community. It was one of the earliest of modern cemeteries.

3
Churchyards: History Since 1700

Around 1700 a significant shift in attitudes to outdoor memorials can be identified. This can be summed up as a growing willingness for persons of social standing to be buried outdoors, and to have imposing memorials raised to their memory. Alongside this, tombs were being erected to an ever wider social range of persons, and the modest headstone entered its greatest period. The Georgian churchyard remains an unsurpassed achievement in terms of historical interest and quality of design.

The urban churchyard was starting to be questioned. The medieval practice of confined and crowned town graveyards was becoming increasingly unpleasant as town populations soared in the years after 1600. John Evelyn had recommended new out-of-town graveyards in his 1666 proposals for the rebuilding of London after the Great Fire: Evelyn liked the idea of building memorials outside the city walls, 'affording a useful diversion to the contemplative passenger of his mortality, and human frailty... as to having that superstitious custom of burying in churches, or having their dormitories in the very heart of cities, where frequently churches are built, I neither think it decent, nor sufferable.' Half a century later, leading architects like Sir Christopher Wren and Sir John Vanbrugh were writing about how best to remember the dead, and how to improve urban life. They were early neoclassicists, wanting to return to the Roman model of imposing outdoor tombs. New churches were being built: where should the graveyards go? Vanbrugh urged a move away from 'little Tawdry Monuments of Marble, stuck up against Walls and Pillars' and hoped that 'lofty and Noble Mausoleums' would arise, in tree-lined, walled cemeteries, to be opened outside built-up areas.

Did you know?

The average country churchyard will contain thousands of bodies, deposited over a millennium or more. Town graveyards can be much fuller: Christ Church, Spitalfields (London Borough of Tower Hamlets), was used between 1729 and 1859, and some 68,000 people were buried there.

One of the very earliest of such cemeteries was opened in Bloomsbury (London) in 1713, to service new churches in Bloomsbury. Now known as St George's Gardens, it contains some large baroque monuments which indicate the growing desire for imposing outdoor tombs. Edinburgh's Greyfriars Kirkyard, opened 150 years before, had shown what the potential was for grandiose outdoor burial in the heart of the city. England was slow in following, and the most impressive eighteenth-century graveyards tended to be suburban ones, where affluent families settled and where they died. Room was often at a premium too in these inner city graveyards, which further discouraged the raising of large memorials. Some urban

Above: St George's Gardens was originally a twin burial ground for new parishes in Bloomsbury (London Borough of Camden). Opened in 1714, it was a new kind of burial space: an Anglican cemetery for parishes without churchyards. It became a public park in the 1880s.

Right: The imposing Baroque churchyard gateway at St Oswald's, Ashbourne (Derbyshire), early eighteenth-century. Symbolic portals of this kind began to appear outside churches in the 1620s. Never common, they sometimes featured deathly imagery which was intended to put the churchgoer in a suitably God-fearing mind.

graveyards followed the Dutch example in erecting elaborate gateways which could carry forbidding memento mori symbolism to put the churchgoer in a God-fearing frame of mind.

Scotland, as noted above, had long disapproved of indoor burials. Some commentators south of the border were starting to question the custom of burial inside churches too. The controversist clergyman Thomas Lewis published a diatribe called *Churches no Charnel-house* in 1726 that was 'an enquiry into the profaneness, indecency and pernicious consequences to the living, of burying the dead in churches and churchyards'. Being buried outdoors was becoming more socially respectable, and masons responded to this new market by creating new sorts of memorials. And at the other end of the spectrum, headstones were beginning to be raised to an ever wider social range.

Georgian England witnessed a flourishing of outdoor tomb-building like no other period. From lowly headstone to opulent mausoleum, masons produced huge quantities of memorials which continue to provide a delightful foil to the even older church building. Divines had long looked at the parish burial grounds and found inspiration among the tombs for their sermons and writings, in particular about the need to remember death. This became an important strain in Anglican devotional verse. 'The Graveyard School' is the name given to those poets (Edward Young, Robert Blair, Thomas Gray and others) who took the reader into the churchyard and urged them to look closely at tomb and earth as

Monument to Sir Oliver Style, Bart. (d. 1702), Wateringbury (Kent). This multi-urned tomb was probably made by the London workshop of Edward Stanton, and shows how outdoor tombs were growing in ambition as families of status opted for outdoor burial.

Franceso Bartolozzi after William Hamilton, *Gray's Elegy* (stipple engraving, 1799). Published in 1751, the 'Elegy' was the most famous poem about churchyard contemplation. (Wellcome Collection)

a form of spiritual preparation for death. Thomas Gray's 'Elegy in a Country Churchyard' was published in 1751 and became the inspiration for centuries of sepulchral pilgrims, seeking spiritual counsel. These proto-romantic explorations of graveyards and ruins became a stock theme in Georgian poetry, and the epitaph became a popular literary form. George Wright described graveyards as 'Wisdom's School' in his 1793 work *Pleasing Melancholy*. A walk among the monuments was an improving pursuit, and this further encouraged the raising of sculpted tombs.

Did you know?

Stoke Poges (Buckinghamshire) is a literary shrine: it was the inspiration for Thomas Gray's 'Elegy in a Country Churchyard' (1751) and he is buried here, beside his mother. In 1799 a neoclassical monument by James Wyatt was erected nearby, to honour Gray and his renowned poem.

The handsome tombstones of early Georgian England frequently depicted death's heads and scenes of decay. Middle class monuments tended to be more neutral in their symbolism, with a greater emphasis on social status and family connection in their inscriptions. How these symbols circulated across the country, and how masons' workshops developed distinctive identities, is an area ripe for further study. Areas blessed with local sources of stone, like the Cotswolds or the slate-yielding areas of Leicestershire, developed remarkable traditions of their own. In some cases, masons signed their works and it is possible to build up a sense of a workshop style: names like George Carter of Epsom (1704–73) and William Staveley of Melton Mowbray (1706–81) emerge from oblivion and remind today's viewer that this was a significant trade, carried out with great accomplishment across the land. While most tombs were conventional in design, some stood out. Some persons left large sums in their will to pay for memorials: none exceeded the opulence of the remarkable tomb at Burton Lazars to William Squire (d. 1786), an opulent concoction of pyramid and sculpture for a modest weaver who left half of his fortune for this monument.

Tombs of classical antiquity had long been a great source of inspiration for architects and masons. In the age of neoclassicism, this became even more the case. Of none was this more true than Sir John Soane (1753–1837), the outstanding architect of his day, whose preoccupation with funereal art of the past resulted in a series of remarkable idiosyncratic churchyard monuments. The numbers of memorials erected across the whole country continued to rise, as an ever-wider range of persons aspired to memorialisation. The majority, however, would still never have had a memorial.

Above left: A fine Baroque tomb in Tetbury churchyard (Gloucestershire), showing the strongly architectural character that the Cotswold school of masons was able to produce.
Avove right: The singular tomb of William Squire (d. 1786), Burton Lazars (Leicestershire). Squire, a modest weaver, left half of his £600 fortune to build and maintain this monument. Statues of Faith and Hope flank an elaborate pierced obelisk. This was originally painted in a faux-marble scheme.

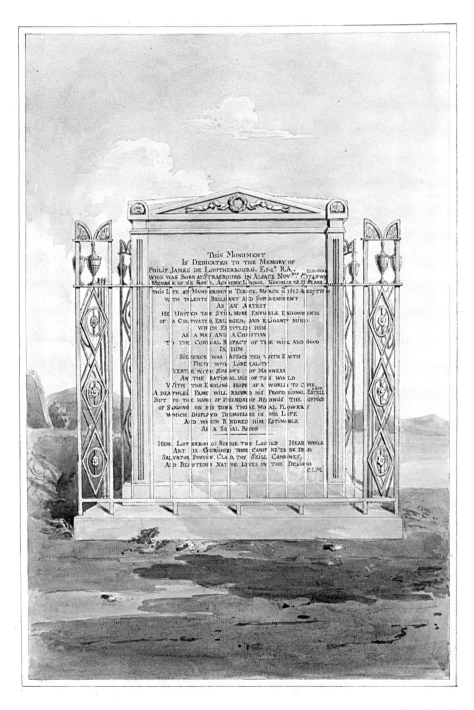

Unknown artist, after Sir John Soane: tomb of Philip Jacques de Loutherbourg (d. 1812), St Nicholas, Chiswick (London Borough of Hounslow). This was one of a series of distinctive tombs by later Georgian Britain's leading architect; de Loutherbourg was a noted painter of dramatic scenes. (Yale Center for British Art)

Did you know?

There is only one Grade I listed churchyard monument in England: the tomb of architect Sir John Soane and his wife, erected in St Pancras Gardens after her death in 1815. The distinctive form of the canopy inspired the design of the K2 telephone kiosk in 1926.

The idea of the churchyard underwent various changes in the nineteenth century. For the rural graveyard, it was a case of returning to presumed modes of medieval piety, and employing the increasingly industrialised trade in memorials to furnish permanent tributes to the dead. Instead of using local materials, however, the nineteenth century saw a huge rise in imported memorial masonry.

Urban churchyards were under greater pressure, triggered by the soaring urban population. By the 1830s, a crisis had been reached in urban burial grounds. A London surgeon, George Walker, published an alarming exposé on the situation called *Gatherings from Grave Yards* (1839). A study of 'the unwise & revolting custom of inhuming the dead in the midst of the living', it led the campaign for sanitary reform, culminating in profound changes in the early 1850s. This brought about the closure of urban burial grounds, and ushered in a nationwide wave of garden cemeteries, run by local public bodies, on the edge of settlements, made necessary by the Burial Acts of 1852–7. After centuries of receiving the urban dead, the town churchyard was coming to the end of its active life. From the 1880s they began to be converted into public parks, which often required the wholesale removal of monuments.

The Gothic Revival of the 1840s onwards placed a renewed emphasis on the sanctity of God's Acre and a revived interest was taken in the upkeep of those graveyards which were still in use. The ideal churchyard, neatly maintained and tended, was seldom a reality. The influential Scottish writer on landscape design John Claudius Loudon published *On the Laying Out, Planting, and Managing of Cemeteries; and on the Improvement of Churchyards* in 1843. It presented a bleak assessment of the situation: 'The intellectual and moral influence which churchyards are calculated to have on the rural population will not, we think, be disputed... few of them are kept in a manner to answer the end proposed, and that a great many are in a state of deplorable neglect'. Loudon's advice was for an altogether more rational approach to be taken to churchyard layout, and to bring them more in line with cemeteries; it is perhaps a good thing that most were left alone. Guidance began to be published on the topic, advising clergymen how to care for them, and suggesting the sort of Christian (as opposed to Pagan) design which might be appropriate for new memorials: William Hastings Kelke's *The Churchyard Manual* (1851), aimed firmly at parish priests who wished to improve the appearance of God's Acre, included designs for medieval revival tombs by the fast-rising architect George Gilbert Scott.

Piety was paralleled by doubts too. Intellectually, the nineteenth century witnessed in some quarters a profound questioning of long-held Christian tenets. Growing evidence for a scientific explanation of evolution, led by Charles Darwin's *On the Origin of Species* (1859), questioned the biblical account of creation; Christians affirm their belief in the resurrection of the dead every time they repeat the Apostles' Creed, but was it literally true? Henry Bowler's painting *Can These Dry Bones Live?* (Tate, 1861) posed the same question as the vision of Ezekiel had done in the Old Testament about the feasibility of bodily re-assembly at the sounding of the Last Trump. Cremation, hitherto illegal, became an issue of live debate

Above left: John Claudius Loudon, *On the Laying Out, Planting, and managing of Cemeteries and on the Improvement of Churchyards* (1843). This influential landscape designer proposed a radical reform of the churchyard, bringing it more in line with the cemeteries which were opening in growing numbers. (Felix Moore)

Above right: Henry Bowler, *The Doubt: 'Can These Dry Bones Live?'* (1855). Bowler's painting showed a visitor to a churchyard pondering the realities of bodily decay. Painted in an age of growing religious anxiety as to the old certainties of resurrection, the painting offered a reassurance in the name on the tombstone – John Faithfull. (Tate)

from the 1870s and became legal from 1884. A millennium on from their establishment, some of the certainties about graveyard burial were starting to be challenged, and the consoling prospect of bodily resurrection was giving way to doubt.

These factors form part of the background to changes in the design of churchyard monuments from the mid-nineteenth century. Larger tombs with brick vaults and kerbs increasingly replaced the traditional headstone and body mound (the earth which traditionally had been raised over a new grave). As a result, churchyards often had to expand as room started to run out. It is a great blessing that older tombs were not cleared away; other countries, which don't have an established tradition of leaving the dead (and their tombs) in place, have lost much of their memorial heritage.

Monuments in general were becoming more standardised, and were increasingly the result of industrial (as opposed to artisanal) production. Improvements in transport made the hitherto expensive movement of stones more affordable, leading to standardisation and the erosion of regional specialities. Granite, long known for its weathering properties, began to be increasingly used and the quarries around Aberdeen exported large volumes. Technology, such as steam power, made cutting and polishing this intractable material more affordable. Other developments, like the invention of lead lettering in 1853, served to erode the bespoke craft aspect of the trade in tombs. Marble, long admired as the quintessential material of classical remembrance, started to be imported in great quantities, and Italian statuary firms were able to supply ready-carved memorials in a number of styles. While this may have made sculpted memorials more affordable, it did introduce a somewhat alien and standardised presence into many rural churchyards. What was suitable for the municipal cemetery wasn't always appropriate for God's Acre, but some fascinating memorials continued to be raised.

All the same, churchyards continued to attract growing numbers of visitors. Jerome K. Jerome's much-loved 1889 satire *Three Men in a Boat* pointed out the strangeness of this practice:

> I don't know whether it is that I am built wrong, but I never did seem to hanker after tombstones myself. I know that the proper thing to do, whenever you get to a village or town, is to rush off and enjoy the graves; but it is a recreation that

The tomb of Sir Henry Morton Stanley (d. 1904) at St Michael and All Angels' churchyard, Pirbright (Surrey). The Welsh-born explorer of Central Africa is remembered with a massive upright stone, crudely dressed and fenced in with craggy posts. An eclectic Edwardian memorial, showing the varied forms taken by some memorials in an age when most were conventional. (Postcard of c. 1910)

I always deny myself. I take no interest in creeping around dim and chilly churches behind wheezy old men, and reading epitaphs.

Some tombstones became the subject of popular postcards, printed in large numbers from the 1890s onwards, to satisfy the rising demand for souvenirs of local sights from tourists.

With the increase in numbers of cemeteries, and the steady rise in numbers of persons being cremated, the traditional idea of the churchyard as the principal place of rest was under attack. Maintenance became a growing issue. In Wales, the Welsh Church Act of 1914 disestablished the Church, placing the care of many graveyards in local authority care; not all authorities accepted this new responsibility, casting them into a legal limbo. At this time also, a reforming spirit affected the carving of tombstones: the mechanised predictability of granite and marble stones started to be challenged by the artist-craftsman.

Eric Gill (1882–1940) led a revival in letter-cutting and direct hand-carving into stone, while the painter-sculptor Gilbert Ledward (1888–1960) founded a firm in 1934 devoted to reviving bespoke, one-off memorials in native stone.

In the mid-twentieth century a crisis of confidence can be sensed in the direction taken in recent times towards churchyard management. The Church of England first issued guidance on graveyards in 1936. The Revd Laurence Harris, in his *Concerning Churchyards* of 1938, wrote of how 'many churchyards are spoiled by ugly and pretentious monuments, rusty iron rails and chains, artificial wreaths under wire guards and a battalion of jam jars. The churchyard should resemble, as far as possible, a quiet and peaceful garden, and the smaller the monuments it contains the better'.

Writers like John Betjeman and Geoffrey Grigson were drawing attention to the splendours of churchyards at this time, and tombstones started to be included in Shell Guides. A travelling exhibition on tombstones was organised for the Arts Council in 1952, organised by the rising expert in the field, an artist named Frederick Burgess. But for many, tombs were regarded as little more than irrelevant curiosities; cultures of maintenance had broken down,

Tombstone to Harry 'Brusher' Mills (d. 1905), St Nicholas church, Brockenhurst (Hampshire). A noted snake-catcher and local curiosity, Mills lived for thirty years in a hut in the New Forest. His marble memorial was visited by many tourists, and it became a popular subject for postcards. (Postcard of 1909)

and caring for churchyards was seldom a priority. Writing in *Country Life* in 1960, Burgess expressed his concern at the trend for clearance:

> Since the war, lack of cheap labour for grass-cutting has driven many parish councils and cemetery authorities to decide that their fetish of tidiness can best be served by rooting up gravestones entirely. What started as precedent is in danger of becoming custom... many churchyard headstones and monuments are being removed and broken up, with little if any protest.

Plenty of regrettable tomb clearances continued to take place in the 1960s, but increasingly Church authorities refused to grant permission for such schemes. And modern gravestones of real quality can show how the tradition lives on.

The times were changing: interest in folk art and local customs was growing, and churchyards began to be more appreciated. Nature conservation in particular championed the graveyard on ecological grounds: the Living Churchyard and Cemetery Project was set up in 1985, later morphing into Caring for God's Acre. Official heritage protection in the form of listing tombs was slow in coming (and remains inconsistent), but in some churchyards, dozens of tombs can be found on the National Heritage List for England. In the twenty-first century, there remains much work to do if Britain's churchyard heritage is to endure; but a corner has certainly been turned.

Levelled tombs at Skipsea (East Yorkshire). In many places in the later twentieth century, the burden of maintenance led to the toppling of tombs to make mowing easier. The impact on the churchyard is readily sensed. Church authorities now discourage such clearance. (Paul Stamper)

Right: Memorial to Diana Blow
(d. 1967) at Wilsford (Wiltshire).
Designed by the architect Roderick
Gradidge (d. 2000), this Aesthetic
Movement-inspired stone shows the
standards modern memorials can
sometimes reach.

Below: The churchyard at Great Tew
(Oxfordshire): eighteenth-century
headstones stand within a wild flower
meadow, a pleasing combination
of nature and sepulchral heritage
reflecting modern conservation
approaches.

4

Tomb Variations

Thomas Rowlandson, 'Dr Syntax among the Tomb Stones' from William Combe's *Dr Syntax in Search of the Picturesque* (etching, 1812). The rise of scholarly interest in Britain's antiquities – including churchyards – comes in here for some prodding humour. (Wikimedia)

Churchyard monuments of the post-medieval period come in plenty of varieties, but there are two standard types: the single block of stone, set upright to form a headstone, and the more complex chest tomb. There are, of course, regional differences which complicate the picture and which arose out of geology and custom. And then there are those exceptional memorials which defy categorisation but which add so much to the thrill of discovery that awaits the graveyard explorer. This chapter looks briefly at the different forms these tombs take, beginning with the simplest and ending up with the most grandiose: from headstone to mausoleum.

The Headstone
The tombstone is the most common sort of outdoor memorial, and one of the splendours of the British craft tradition. Easy to produce, and secure when sunk deep enough into the ground, these single slabs of stone marked the site of the grave and were generally placed at the head end; sometimes smaller stones bearing initials and dates were added at the foot end, and are thus called footstones. The size of these tombstones can vary considerably,

Above left: The double headstone to Thomas and Susanna Godfrey (d. 1665), St Mary of Charity church, Faversham (Kent). This distinctive hump-backed kind of memorial was a speciality of seventeenth-century Kent.

Above right: An unidentified Scottish headstone at Dryburgh Abbey (Borders) from the early eighteenth century, emphasising the deceased person's studious or pious character. Portraits are not frequently encountered on headstones of any period.

in thickness and in height: geology determines some of the dimensions, as slate can be worked very thin and some sandstones have to be very thick. One area which developed a distinct tombstone tradition early on was Kent: its distinctive hump backed stones, sometimes paired, were carved from sandstone and could contain stylised death's heads. Scotland, with its disapproval of indoor commemoration, also produced a vigorous and highly distinctive tradition from the sixteenth century onwards, using locally available sandstones to create heavily modelled designs which, even when no longer identifiable, connect today's viewer with past lives in a very immediate way.

Early headstones show classically influenced designs in the seventeenth century, and then advances to more exuberant – even baroque – shapes and decoration in the early eighteenth, often with richly scrolled frames to the edges. In the mid-eighteenth century there is a move to more delicate designs, sometimes curvaceously rococo in style, and later neoclassical, displaying a move away from the imagery of mortality into a gentler,

5. John Peel's Grave, Caldbeck.

Above left: Unidentified headstone of c. 1740 at the church of St Thomas the Apostle, Lymington (Hampshire). At the top, angels open a draped canopy to reveal the Lamb of God; the scrolled frame below provided some worldly elegance.

Above right: Headstone to Thomas Waterfall (d. 1747), St Lawrence's church, Little Stanmore (London Borough of Harrow). This exuberantly carved Portland stone memorial is fashionably rococo in its decorative treatment.

Left: The renowned huntsman John Peel (d. 1859) was buried in St Kentigern's churchyard, Caldbeck (Cumbria). A late example of a Greek revival headstone, it includes a hound, hunting horns and whips – symbols of his career in the field. (Postcard of c. 1910)

more decorative mode. Later Georgian headstones tended to be plainer, with a greater emphasis on inscription rather than imagery. In the Victorian epoch (from 1837), many headstones continued to be erected in this enduring classical style, such as the well-known stone to Lakelands huntsman John Peel (d. 1859). By then, however, the Gothic Revival had started to question the appropriateness of these pagan sorts of memorials, and there was a return to the crosses, ledger stones and other medieval forms thought appropriate in God's Acre. Sometimes these were made from new, industrial materials like terracotta; others were made from granite or marble, which were made more affordable by improved transport links and new stone-cutting technology.

One of the joys of the headstone is its combination of word and image, of decorative lettering with symbolism. Leicestershire's notable tradition of slate produced gravestones of the first order: decorative, clear, long-lasting and dignified, these stones were exported across the country using the new canal network for ease of transportation. Another slate-yielding area, Cornwall, produced stones of a very different character; not until the nineteenth century is a standardisation evident on tombstones. Victorian and later headstones could still be eclectic, but there was a much greater homogeneity, broadly speaking. Some twentieth-century tombstones paid deliberate homage to the Georgian tradition.

Below left: A late Victorian terracotta grave-marker at St James the Great, Radley (Oxfordshire). The Gothic Revival meets industrial production; the inscription would have been cut onto a marble panel, which has disappeared. (Nick Wright)

Below right: Improvements in the transport network enabled stones to be carried more cheaply across the country: this fine Leicestershire slate headstone to Sarah Wheatley (d. 1790) was probably brought by canal to the great Dissenter burial ground of Bunhill Fields (London Borough of Islington).

Above left: Tombstone at Cardinham (Cornwall) to John Stevens (d. 1785). Regional distinctiveness and rural craftsmanship provide much of the joy to be derived from British memorials.
Above right: Tombstone of the American painter Edwin Austin Abbey (d. 1911), St Andrew's old church, Kingsbury (London Borough of Brent). This was a precise copy of a 1740 tombstone in the same churchyard, carved by the eminent sculptor Sir Thomas Brock: a clear tribute to the esteem Georgian memorials were held in.

Did you know?

The tombstone most often found in churchyards is that erected by the Imperial (now Commonwealth) Graves Commission, founded in 1917. The distinctive design, usually in Portland stone, was designed by a committee led by the Director of the British Museum, Sir Frederic Kenyon.

The twentieth century witnessed the increasing commercialisation of the monumental mason's trade: with this came standardisation, industrial manufacture (such as the use of air-compressed sand-blasting and pneumatic chisels), imported materials and, all too often, a dropping away of aesthetic standards. In contrast, there was also a return to wooden grave-markers in some places too. By far the most commonly encountered headstone in British churchyards is the handsome tribute erected by the Imperial (since 1960, Commonwealth) War Graves Commission. Laser-etched portraits cut into black granites became a common form of memorial from the 1990s. Church authorities have long promoted native stones for historic churchyards, and in recent decades there has been a revival in standards,

Above left: The headstone to Sgt John Hannah VC (d. 1947), Birstall (Leicestershire). Erected by the Imperial War Graves Commission, this stone honoured a very brave airman who was badly burnt trying to put out an on-board fire in 1940. These stones were mass-produced but not at the expense of dignity and enduring quality.

Above right: Headstones in the Jewish burial ground, Falmouth (Cornwall). This lies outside the town, and adjoins a Congregationalist burial ground. Only the Hebrew inscriptions, and Jewish dates, differentiate these stones from other local slate memorials.

spearheaded by the influential body Memorials by Artists. The tombstone tradition has not withered, but actually shows signs of a revival – for those who can afford it.

Other faith groups beside Anglicans have erected very similar headstones: only the inscriptions mark them apart. At Falmouth (Cornwall), one of the more remote Jewish burial grounds lies on the edge of town and contains a few dozen tombstones, some signed by local Cornish masons.

Bodystones and Coffin Stones

These two related forms started to appear between head and footstones towards the end of the eighteenth century, and are most commonly found in the London area. They are interesting psychologically, as they replicate the body shape or burial beneath, and mark the physicality of human remains. Bodystones are vaguely anthropomorphic, whereas coffin stones could depict actual caskets with some accuracy: a good example of such, complete with carved handles, is at Maldon, Essex. The best-known bodystones are at Cooling (Kent), which are said to have inspired the graveyard scene in Charles Dickens' *Great Expectations* (1861).

Coffins started to appear in the place of effigies on some church monuments (as in Derby Cathedral) in the mid-seventeenth century. Bodies would have been carried to the grave in coffins,

Tomb of William Raymond (d. 1812), All Saints, Maldon, Essex. This tomb fuses the body and coffin-stone types, and provides a detailed depiction of a smart, ornamented coffin.

and generally (though not always) buried in them too. There are a few examples of early eighteenth-century outdoor coffin-shaped stones with added macabre decoration, as though the shape itself was not sombre enough. At Baslow (Derbyshire), Robin Stafford (d. 1702) lies beneath just one such tomb, decorated with a skull.

Graveboards

Sometimes called dead-boards, these consist of wooden boards, set between upright posts. Often originally painted, these affordable memorials were once found in some numbers in some south-eastern areas such as Surrey, Hertfordshire and Buckinghamshire, where stone memorials were more costly. A very splendid specimen is in Hampstead churchyard (London Borough of Camden) to artist and playwright George Du Maurier (d. 1896), embellished with copper sheathing. Most have rotted away, making their survival quite special. These were the last common form of wooden churchyard memorials, and thus form a link with the centuries-old tradition of temporary timber grave-markers.

Tomb of George Du Maurier (d. 1896), St John-at-Hampstead, London Borough of Camden. This is an exceptionally ornate example of the once-common grave-board kind of memorial, embellished with neo-Celtic ornament and protected by copper flashing.

Ledger Slabs

A ledger slab is a flat stone, generally resting on a low brick or masonry plinth around the grave shaft. Prestigious burial inside churches had, for centuries, been marked by the placing of inscribed slabs over the burial vault. Transferring this over to the churchyard maintained a degree of exclusivity to the vault space: the dead remained protected by these heavy covers, and their precise place of rest was identified and secured. Ledger slabs needed to be of durable stone: limestone was generally too prone to weathering, but the strong millstone grits of Yorkshire proved ideal, and could receive lettering easily too on account of their fine grain. Ledger slabs are thus commonly encountered in northern England, and the horizontal character of some northern churchyards is very marked and distinctive. These became more common in southern England from the later eighteenth century, because canal transport was lowering the costs of delivery. Plain they may be, but their sheer size can still be impressive. Coped ledger stones, a medieval form with raised ridges along their length, were popular in the Gothic Revival: the architect G. F. Bodley (d. 1907) has one such at Kinnersley.

Above: A view of the churchyard of St Peter's, Leeds (Yorkshire). The ground is covered in heavy late Georgian ledger stones; writhing tree roots push them upwards.

Left: The celebrated church architect George Frederick Bodley (1827–1907) was celebrated for his mastery of Gothic design. He was buried at Kinnersley (Herefordshire) beneath a slab (on the right) which echoed medieval grave covers.

An unidentified table tomb at Corsham (Wiltshire), probably of c. 1800. Clearly to a soldier, it shows how the table tomb could be adapted into a fashionable neoclassical style. The cover protected the carved urn, which remains in good condition.

Table Tombs

Half way between the raised ledger slab and the chest tomb is the table tomb – known in Scotland as the tablestone. As the name implies, this is a table-like design with a flat cover borne up by upright supports at the corners. These could be quite low, as numerous examples in the North demonstrate; elsewhere they were raised up quite high, like protective canopies above the vault, and their descent from internal canopy tombs is clear to see. The form was an enduring one. At Corsham (Wiltshire), a neoclassical table tomb, sadly without inscription, protects an urn enriched with military trophies.

Chest Tombs and Sarcophagi

Chest tombs are simple constructions: four-sided boxes on top of a sub-structure, with a slab on top. They echoed the above-ground receptacles in which certain prestigious burials took place inside churches: outside, burials tended to take place below ground, and not inside the chests themselves. Medieval examples are quite numerous. Tudor and Stuart examples can be hard to date, because inscriptions have so often weathered away. At West Tarring (West Sussex), the tomb of John Parson (d. 1633) has retained its lettering very well, including an early outdoor epitaph. A more sophisticated example, showing how the style of

Above: Tomb of John Parson (d. 1633), West Tarring (West Sussex). This simply constructed but hardy chest tomb is remarkable for the survival of its inscriptions. One reads: 'Youth was his age: / Virginity his state: / Learning his love: / Consumption his fate'.

Below: Canopy tombs at Dyserth churchyard (Denbighshire); this distinctively Welsh tomb variant used local sandstone to great effect. Lower table tombs stand close by. (Maddy Gray)

the indoor monument was being brought outdoors, is at Wateringbury (Kent), where Henry Wood (d. 1630) was buried. This was a new form of chest tomb, with deathly carvings on the pilasters of the chest, and a long epitaph. A distinctive Welsh variant consisted of chest tombs with arched canopies above: a spectacular pair exists at Dyserth to members of the Hughes family of likely seventeenth-century date, standing alongside lower table tombs.

The mid-seventeenth century was a significant time for the expansion of outdoor tomb types. In the Midlands, chests with single or double-coped slabs are found: these twin-peaked tombs are rather touching embodiments of married couples being laid to rest together. In the Cotswolds, the 'bale tomb' emerged in the later seventeenth century, its name coming from the resemblance between this kind of chest tomb's rounded top and bales of wool (from which so much of the region's wealth derived).

The most common form of chest tomb found in England has moulded corners with baluster-like panels; inscriptions were cut into slabs on top. Initially forming part of indoor church monuments and designed by the eminent mason Nicholas Stone, the type became widely deployed outdoors and lasted about 200 years. Variants on this design are legion. At Grantham (Lincolnshire), the tomb of Ann Huthwaite (d. 1760) consists of a chest with dramatically waisted end panels, showing how the language of masonry components could be altered to produce a striking twist on conventional tomb design.

If these tombs have a drawback, it is their tendency to fall apart (something we look at in Chapter 7). One eminent early Georgian mason knew exactly how to build for eternity. Christopher Cass (d. 1734), was Master Mason to the Ordnance (the branch of government

Tombs in the churchyard of St Michael, Wadenhoe (Northamptonshire); among the tombstones are several twin-gabled chest tombs from the seventeenth century, a regional variation on this emerging type of tomb.

Left: Chest tomb of William Hart (d. 1717), St John at Hampstead (London Borough of Camden). A fine example of the angle baluster chest tomb, one of the most common varieties of the larger sort of outdoor tomb. Monuments like this were erected in the seventeenth to nineteenth centuries.

Below: Mrs Ann Huthwaite monument (d. 1760), St Wulfram's church, Grantham (Lincolnshire). The boldness of the curved end panels show how the conventional chest tomb could be varied by an inventive mason.

responsible for building for and supplying the Army), and his own monument, in the St John's burial ground, Horseferry Road, Westminster, was designed to last. Not only was it made from Cornish granite (a very early non-local use of this durable but difficult to work material), it was also designed in massive forms with deeply incised lettering which would withstand decay. Few other tomb designers heeded his example.

Sarcophagus, from the Greek words for flesh eater, is the term given to a chest tomb with a pronounced classical character. These may be decorated with strigillation, the repeated s-bend ornament derived from Roman skin scrapers. Others sport acroteria, or decorative finials, or have pedimented covers; the name for the smaller, tapering chests on ball-feet is an arca. Like the urn, this originally funereal classical symbol became very popular in the neoclassical period throughout the decorative arts.

Christopher Cass (d. 1734) was Master Mason to His Majesty's Board of Ordnance and knew a great deal about the weathering properties of stones, and how to build to last. His own granite tomb in the St John's Burial Ground, Horseferry Road (City of Westminster), has done just that.

Tomb of William Praed (d. 1833), Lelant (Cornwall). Prominently located just outside the east end of St Uny's church, this is an elegant example of the neoclassical sarcophagus which retains its railings. Outdoor burial was becoming increasingly the norm for all classes.

Pedestal Tombs

Chest tombs are rectangular and horizontal: pedestal tombs are emphatically upright. Generally square in plan, they are classical in character and sometimes support objects like urns. A grand and early example is at Richmond (Surrey), dating from around 1700, to Lady Bowyer: this one has a large urn, guarded by sentinel putti, all very much in the baroque spirit, showing how the preferences of indoor tombs were being transferred to

The Copley Monument of c. 1700 (St Mary Magdalene church, Richmond-upon-Thames, London). Erected in memory of his mother, Lady Bowyer, Sir John Copley commissioned a lavish baroque pedestal tomb of marble; this stone has suffered badly, but was consolidated in 2005.

Pedestal tombs in St Mary's churchyard, Arlingham (Gloucestershire). Here is a fine group of later Georgian outdoor tombs, continuing the Cotswold tradition of sepulchral display.

churchyard monuments; the decision to use marble in an outdoor setting was not wise, however, as it has decayed. Pedestal tombs became a staple in the Georgian churchyard, and occasionally were made of material other than stone, such as cast iron. There were many variations which blurred the distinction between the chest tomb and the pedestal tomb: sometimes they are called tea caddy tombs because they resemble the ornate vessels which graced polite tables. The Cotswold region made a particular specialism of such designs; Arlingham, on the banks of the Severn, has an exceptionally fine collection.

Columns, Obelisks and Pyramids

Columns and obelisks are even more emphatically vertical, standing head and shoulders above normal tombs to ensure immediate recognition in the churchyard. The first memorial mentioned in the Bible was the pillar raised over Rachel's grave by Jacob in the Book of Genesis: early modern instances of column monuments can be found, but the outstanding example dates from the mid-eighteenth century, when the renowned mason-turned-architect Sir Robert Taylor raised a marble column of gratitude to the Godfrey family. Half-columns became a common form of memorial in the later Georgian period: sometimes they were deliberately truncated, to indicate a fracture in lineage. At Richmond (North Yorkshire), a magnificent High Victorian classical column with full entablature above stands in St Mary's churchyard; symbols on the base show this to have been inspired by Freemasonry.

Below left: Sir Robert Taylor: column to the Godfrey family (after 1763), St Mary, South Woodford (London Borough of Redbridge). The grandest example of a column tomb, erected by an eminent architect in tribute to a family which had been very supportive of his career early on.
Below right: Obelisk to Thomas Falconer (d. 1729), St George's Gardens (London Borough of Camden). This is one of the largest early Georgian memorials anywhere; Falconer had made much money in India and died soon after his return to London.

One of the oddest British churchyard memorials is the pyramidal mausoleum to John Fuller MP (d. 1811) at Brightling (Sussex). Built by a local mason called Smythe in 1810, it shows the fascination for ancient Egypt of the day, and the appetite for funereal display. The belief that 'Mad Jack' was buried in a seated position has been disproved. (Wikimedia)

Obelisks had started to appear as secular monuments in the early eighteenth century, and had long been features on internal church monuments. An early appearance of an outdoor obelisk tomb, and on a heroic scale too, can be found in the Bloomsbury burial ground now called St George's Gardens, erected in memory of Thomas Falconer, who died in 1729, not long after his return from India. Obelisks are shafts topped with small pyramids: larger pyramids were occasionally used for family tombs, as at Painswick. The mightiest churchyard example is at Brightling (Sussex), built in 1811, where it marks the resting place of John Fuller MP. Perhaps no other kind of memorial was further removed from the traditional Christian forms as this one.

Crosses

Medieval churchyards frequently had crosses in their midst, casting a protective holiness above the graves of the dead. Cross-shaped memorials to individuals were unusual before the Gothic Revival, and only started to become common in the later nineteenth century, with the rise of the imported Italian marble memorial. Because of its pious tradition and prominent height, the cross was revived by some Victorian designers and masons. Heavy Celtic crosses of granite became a staple among cemetery memorials, and towards the close

Above left: A design of 1850 for a churchyard memorial at Malpas (Cheshire), by Samuel Cranston of Hereford. The Gothic Revival sought to replace classical and pagan forms of monument with evidently Christian tributes to faith. (Author's collection)

Above right: Guy Dawnay MP was gored to death by a buffalo in East Africa in 1889. He was remembered with an elegant slender cross at Great Bookham (Surrey) which fused the churchyard cross tradition with a heraldic tribute to his noble family.

of the nineteenth century churchyards began to receive more and more such monuments; Italian marble crosses embellished with anchors and ivy (more associated with cemeteries than churchyards) became popular too. Others were more bespoke, and could attain high levels of gracefulness.

Sculpted Tombs

Sculpture generally does not fare well in outdoor situations. Although outdoor medieval effigies were not unusual, they did become very rare in the post-Reformation period. Carving was restricted to small-scale reliefs, with occasionally more florid and projecting figures to tombs, particularly in the Cotswold area. One highly unusual exception to this is at Stonham Aspall (Suffolk), where leading London mason Francis Bird carved a semi-reclining effigy of Anthony Wingfield (d. 1715) upon a bulbous sarcophagus; it has not weathered well, showing how such tombs are better kept inside. A happier example is found at Finchley churchyard, where a poignant figure graces the monument of Mrs Elizabeth Norris (d. 1777). Some modern tombs use sculpture to perpetuate memory. The art critic Peter Fuller was tragically killed in an accident in 1990 (together with his unborn son); Glynn Williams carved a stylised chestnut bud for his memorial, symbolising nature's power of regeneration.

Above: At Stonham Aspall (Suffolk) is the very unusual outdoor effigy to Anthony Wingfield (d. 1715). The concept is that of an indoor memorial, and its sculptor, Francis Bird, carved many such tombs for Westminster Abbey. Lichens have transformed the appearance of the figure. (C. B. Newham)

Left: Glynn Williams: tomb of Peter Fuller and son (d. 1990). Fuller, a celebrated art critic, is remembered with a bold sculpture at Stowlangtoft (Suffolk), depicting nature's powers of regeneration.

The Mausoleum

Larger than a tomb, a mausoleum is a structure devoted to housing the dead. Named after Mausolus, a ruler in fourth-century BC Asia Minor whose death led to the construction of a huge sepulchre at Halicarnassus, one of the wonders of the ancient world, these buildings are the acme of commemorative grandeur. Some early mausolea were built by aristocrats in private grounds, to avoid clerical control: the Howard Mausoleum at Castle Howard (North Yorkshire), designed by Nicholas Hawksmoor and completed in 1736, remains the mightiest example of the type. Burial in consecrated ground was an important consideration for most, however, so the majority of mausolea were erected in churchyards.

Georgian examples tended to be classical in style. At Farningham (Kent), the Nash family raised a small building of Portland stone as their mausoleum in 1785, an obelisk on top forming a funereal finial to drive home its sepulchral function. Inside is a domed chamber with inscription tablets, and a series of stone shelves called loculi, on which lead coffins were placed, and then sealed in with stone covers. Mausolea enabled bodies to be kept above ground, rather than buried: they had to be embalmed and placed in multi-layered coffins, a further sign of the exclusivity which characterises the mausoleum. Victorian mausolea were sometimes classical, sometimes Egyptian, but more often Gothic in style. Mausolea were erected in some numbers in Victorian cemeteries, but were rarer in churchyards. A very unusual (and small-scale) example of an Arts and Crafts-inflected mausoleum is at Rodborough (Gloucestershire), to house the industrialist Sir Alfred Apperly (d. 1913).

Above and right: The Nash Mausoleum at Farningham (Kent). Built in 1785, it is an elegant neoclassical structure to house the family dead; the obelisk-finial on the roof is an unusual feature and reinforces the funereal nature of the building.

Memorial to Sir Alfred Apperly (d. 1913), Rodborough (Gloucestershire). Not quite mausoleum, but more than a monument, this Arts and Crafts structure combines Christian and pagan symbolism: angels guard the tomb while the swastika is an ancient reference to good fortune. (Photo: David O'Driscoll)

It incorporates a relief of angels flanking a chalice, but with Indian imagery too in the form of the swastika and the woven screen beneath their wings: a reminder that religion in the early twentieth century was increasingly looking at other faiths for inspiration. The form of this memorial, guarding an entrance into an earthen chamber, may well have been suggested by prehistoric long barrows of the kind which survive in the local area. This looking around for nearby inspiration, and adapting ancient forms for contemporary use, were characteristics of the Arts and Crafts movement. Mausolea in churchyards declined as a funeral form in the twentieth century, as modesty in death became more of the norm, and church authorities asserted their right to control burials in their graveyards.

5
Messages to Eternity: Epitaphs and Symbols

The tomb presents the attempt by mourners to keep the dead person in mind, and to stave off the threat of oblivion. Churchyard memorials have a physical presence, identifying the body's resting place. The dead are not the audience of a tomb: that consists of the mourners, and posterity. Through inscriptions and through visual imagery, they broadcast messages about the dead person's life and their faith. Deciphering these is one of the pleasures of the churchyard. Very often, it is the more provincial modest headstones which displayed the most striking imagery.

Lettering

Monuments are communications, and when their inscriptions become illegible, they lose much of their power. Internal monuments had long borne lengthy messages, carefully cut. Outdoor tombs often had shorter inscriptions, cut more deeply to try to last longer. Some early tombstones are remarkable in showing the emergence of literacy: at Newtown

Linford (Leicestershire), John Boney (d. 1683) has a memorable slate stone with abandoned attempts at Latin, and some wayward but wonderful lettering. Standards rose very high later on, as masons absorbed the art of penmanship: slate in particular, which is very fine-grained, could receive very delicate letter-cutting. Not all stones were suitable for having letters cut into them: in the Cotswolds, many limestone tombs had brass plaques set into them, which endured far better. Cast-iron memorials were industrial products,

Slate headstone to John Boney (d. 1683) at Newtown Linford (Leicestershire). This is very special for showing the emergence of literacy on a modest memorial. The opening letters 'HICK JA' was an attempt at the Latin tomb inscription *Hic jacet*, 'Here lies'.

Detail of the cast iron tomb at Baldock (Hertfordshire) to Ann Clarkson (d. 1830); when maintained and repainted, such memorials can retain their legibility very well.

most popular in the early nineteenth century, and part of their appeal was enduring legibility. Modern lettering can attain the highest standards: Simon Verity's slate tombstone for Sir John Betjeman (d. 1984) at St Enodoc's church, Trebetherick (Cornwall), delights in Gothic ornament and celebrates the poet's sparkling character in graphic form.

Epitaphs

Inscribing letters on a tomb help to preserve the fundamentals of identity: a name. The word epitaph derives from the Greek words *epi* and *taphos*, meaning words upon a tomb. Brief details about family, and dates of birth and death, form the essentials but many tombstones give more, with pious verses, or details of the causes of death. Some verses were used over and over again ('Afflictions sore long time he bore, / Physicians were in vain' etc.), while others were bespoke. Some epitaphs were very prolix: few exceed that of John Baylie (d. 1777), a simpleton servant at Stratfield Saye, held in such affection that funds were raised to record his qualities after his death in a splendid verse which included mention of his fondness for gin. Others record less happy lives. Amongst the saddest tombstones anywhere in Britain is the Unknown Sailor stone at Thursley, recording a cruel killing in 1786. Both of these stones have been re-cut in more recent times and purged of lichen to ensure that their messages go on being heard. 'Murder stones' can be found across the British Isles: among the earliest is that to William Mansbridge (d. 1703) at Eling (Hampshire). Victorian epitaphs tended to the conventional and familial, trends which have only intensified in the twentieth century.

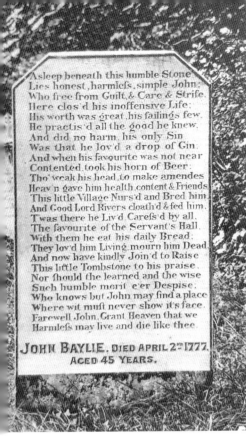

Above left: Tombstone of John Baylie (d. 1777), Stratfield Saye (Hampshire). This re-cut inscription celebrates the life of 'Simple John' whose 'only sin / was that he lov'd a drop of gin'. (Postcard of 1908)
Above right: The tomb of the Unknown Sailor (d. 1786), Thursley (Surrey). This remarkable stone, re-carved in 1955, shows the murder scene, together with an affecting inscription. Modern research suggests he may have been called Edward Hardman.

Did you know?

At Henbury (Bristol) is the celebrated tomb of Scipio Africanus (d. 1720), an African boy slave who became an English aristocrat's servant. Head and footstones have been renewed and re-painted: a reminder that many headstones were once kept bright. A dramatic reminder of a short but special life, showing how tombstones shed light on the past.

Piety

Post-Reformation memorials were careful about depicting sacred images: depictions of Bibles and prayer books were common, but representations of sacred symbols were generally rarer. Adam and Eve, the victims of temptation and responsible for the Fall of Man, were often depicted on Scottish tombstones in particular: 'Adam and Eve by eating the forbidden tree / Brought all mankind to sin and misery' is the inscription beneath one such scene of 1737 at Fettercairn (Aberdeenshire). Depictions of the Saviour, Jesus Christ, generally came later.

Tombstone of Elizabeth Richardson (d. 1829), St Augustine's church, Alston (Cumbria). An unusual relief, showing Christ in the act of blessing: a reflection of the late Georgian evangelical movement.

In St Augustine's churchyard, Alston (Cumbria), is the weathered sandstone tomb of Elizabeth Richardson (d. 1829), with a relief of the Saviour blessing a chalice; much more common was Christ's inclusion in resurrection scenes. The anchor of hope, the cross of faith, angels and crowns of life all became popular symbols on Victorian memorials.

Resurrection and Judgment

Belief in the resurrection of the body was one of the great consolations of Christian faith. Tombstones representing the Last Judgment, when trumpets would sound and the dead arise to life ever after, anticipated this overcoming of mortality on the very spot where the dead would arise. Trumpets awakening the dead were common symbols. One of the most celebrated internal monuments of the eighteenth century was Roubiliac's epic resurrection tomb for General Hargreaves (d. 1764) in Westminster Abbey: numerous provincial monuments echoed its toppling pyramid on modest headstones. The resurrection of the dead was an intricate topic to carve, and many such reliefs are now very weathered. At Broadwater (Sussex), the scarce-legible headstone of Elizabeth Penfold (d. 1793) shows Christ in majesty, flanked by tombs opening up in a churchyard, and a rare scene of bodies surfacing at sea. By this time, tombs were becoming more evasive about the realities of death, and more decorative in character. Cherubim were common features on Georgian tombstones, and their presence was a cheering one, alluding to the life hereafter and to the immortality of the soul.

John Hind (mason): slate tombstone of Thomas and Elizabeth Carrick (d. 1741 and 1755), Blaby (Leicestershire). The relief shows lightning and the last trumpets, awakening the dead from their graves, alongside a censer. The resurrection of the body was an important consolation for mourners. (Elizabeth Blood)

Mortality

Skulls and crossbones start to appear on outdoor tombs in the seventeenth century, and this stark symbol of death became a common one on early Georgian tombs across Britain. The message of the memento mori is obvious: by stressing the finiteness of existence, tombs could drive home the message of the need to lead a God-fearing life. Symbolic skeletons brought death to life. They were tricky to carve, and deliberately fearsome (particularly in an age in which images were so much scarcer than they were to become later). Death could form a pair, with Father Time: the hour of death was always approaching, and time was ever shorter. Father Time could be as frightening as Death sometimes, a spiteful presence eager to bring lives to their close. Some stones include poignant portraits of the deceased,

Unidentified memorial of *c.* 1700 at Melrose Abbey (Borders); the death's head was long a ubiquitous symbol of mortality, but had become rare by 1800.

Above: Unidentified chest tomb of *c.* 1720 at St Nicholas churchyard, Standish (Gloucestershire), showing Time (with scythe) and Death (with dart). There was to be no escaping the reaper. **Left**: A remarkable depiction of Father Time, pouring out the grains of his hourglass on a portrait of the (unidentified) deceased person, buried within this neoclassical chest tomb of *c.* 1800 at Stilton (Cambridgeshire). (Paul Stamper)

Tombstone of Thomas Guthrie (d. 1792), All Saints' church, Newcastle-upon-Tyne. Scenes showing the decomposition of the body and its reduction to bones were not uncommon in early Georgian tomb reliefs: this is a late example, urging the viewer to 'Remember Death. Think every day your last'.

laid out in shrouds, as at Desborough in Northamptonshire, from 1796. One early Georgian image often found on tombstones was of bone-strewn ground, with skulls emerging from the soil. These took the very graveyard as their subject, but often showed cherubim hovering above: the body might perish, but the soul would live on, and would one day the two would be reunited. This Christian optimism needs to be remembered when looking at grisly Georgian tombstones, which stand over the actual place of burial and decay. Grim their message may have been, and harsh the bluntness with which the realities of bodily dissolution were depicted, but there is a fascination in the carving of these tombstones which is curiously life-affirming.

Love and Loss

Grieving husbands and wives sometimes channelled their loss into memorials which represented their sorrow: the figure of the mourning woman became one of the most popular subjects in neoclassical art, appearing on teapots as well as tombstones. One singular and moving stone of 1781, at Langley (Buckinghamshire), showed a mourning dove, looking onto a sinking sun. Holding hands became a common symbol on later Victorian tombs. A common symbol of rupture was the broken column. One small tombstone at Burwell (Cambridgeshire) tells a heart-breaking tale of village tragedy. Here, the flaming heart is not

Above left: Tombstone of Elizabeth Hitchcock (d. 1781) at St Mary's, Langley (Buckinghamshire). She died aged thirty-four; her sorrowing husband is shown as a mourning dove, watching his sun set. The cherub above alludes to the life hereafter.
Above right: Tombstone of the seventy-eight persons killed when a barn they were inside, while watching a puppet show, caught fire in 1727: St Mary's churchyard, Burwell (Cambridgeshire). The stone was re-cut in 1910.

a Catholic devotional symbol, but a reference to the fire in 1727 which claimed the lives of seventy-eight people, shut into a barn to watch a puppet show, and which then caught fire, leading to a dreadful Fenland tragedy.

Tributes to Careers
Some tombstones proudly celebrated careers and achievements. At Cobham (Kent), one Georgian chest tomb commemorating a prosperous yeoman is capped with a bushel of wheat, while nearby a headstone has a busy relief showing tree-felling and a carpenter's tools. Scottish tombstones in particular included references to trades: at Old Calton burial ground in Edinburgh, Captain John Gray raised a stone to his parents (d. 1747 and 1752), but showed his own vessel in pride of place. Military memorials are legion. One example must suffice: at St Michael's, Iveresk (Midlothian), is a fine memorial to Major Ramsay, an artillery officer, killed at Waterloo. Soldiers' tombstones can yield surprises: in St Nicholas' churchyard,

Brighton (Sussex) is the tombstone of Phoebe Hessel (d. 1821), who died in her 108th year, having 'served for many years as a private Soldier in the 5th Regt. of Foot in different parts of Europe'. Epitaphs are literally messages from the dead.

Right: Tombstone of Richard Gransden (d. 1760), St Mary's, Cobham (Kent). This headstone shows the tools of the carpenter and a scene of tree-felling; such glimpses into past lives and artisanal careers give some tombstones an added value.
Below: Monument to Major William Ramsay (d. 1815), Inveresk parish kirkyard, Midlothian. Ramsay was an artillery officer who served from 1799; at his earlier request, his remains were brought back from the battlefield to join his wife's. (Kim Traynor, via Geograph)

Lychgates

Lychgates are named from the old English word *lic*, for corpse. They are symbolic structures, in the sense of being the receiving points for the dead body as it leaves its old social world behind: once over the threshold, it enters the sacred zone of the church for burial and eternal rest. Most were built of wood, and dated from the late Middle Ages. Some still have coffin rests, where the body could be placed until the final procession was ready to form up. The Gothic Revival of the nineteenth century led to widespread construction of lychgates, often in stone with elaborate timber canopies. At Gwythian, in Cornwall, Edmund Sedding designed the lychgate and created a coffin rest in this spirit of renewed piety.

Remembering the fallen of the First World War led to a final wave of lychgate construction: the names of the parish dead were inscribed on these shelters, and this presence, passed every time parishioners attended church, served to lessen their permanent absence. At St Faith's church, Overbury (Worcestershire), Sir Herbert Baker designed a lychgate in 1921 in memory of the parish's dead; one of its inscriptions reads: 'Through the gate of death we pass to our joyful resurrection', and the Cenotaph-like coffin-rest, on which the names of the dead are inscribed, sports the rousing words of William Blake's 'Jerusalem'. One of the last memorial gateways of note was built at Holy Trinity, Bosham (West Sussex), designed by the famous architect Grey Wornum in memory of his daughter Jenefer, who had drowned in 1950.

Lychgate at St Gwithian's church, Gwythian (Cornwall) by Edmund Sedding, 1865–7, reusing medieval fabric; the coffin rest incorporates a thirteenth-century grave-slab. Cornwall has an exceptional heritage of churchyard structures.

6
Caring for Churchyards

Tombs decay, and yet life goes on. That is one of the comforting messages of time spent in a churchyard. But there is a balance to be struck between letting nature take its course and making sure that historic tombs survive for as long as possible. In many places, particularly in remote rural parishes, caring for the church alone is enough of a challenge.

Parishes formerly would employ a sexton. This virtually extinct profession involved graveyard maintenance and building oversight: the word is derived from sacristanus, or guardian of holy objects. After 1945, the desire to keep churchyards neat and easy to mow led to widespread tomb clearance, which has damaged the character of a good many churchyards. Nowadays they are largely left alone. Nature can flourish in these places, and the organisation Caring for God's Acre is the vanguard of promoting this approach of light-touch management. Bio-diversity thrives when manicured tidiness is set aside, and around 6,000 churchyards are thought to be managed for their wildlife diversity. Lichens flourish on headstones, bringing a new kind of life to these places of remembrance; however, they can secrete acids which affect the surface of the stones they colonise.

Did you know?

Churchyard yews are Britain's oldest trees. Just how old is speculation, but some have stood over 2,000 years. Rivals for the oldest include those at Fortingall (Perthshire) and at St Cynog's, Defynnog, north of Swansea (Powys).

Churchyards are more than collections of tombs, and places of burial over repeated centuries. They contain remarkable trees and are precious spaces for wildlife, as well as containing special structures related to many aspects of parish life. This small heritage-focused book cannot begin to cover all of the aspects of natural interest, yet one of the most enjoyable qualities of a graveyard is the fusion of the man-made with the natural.

If sympathetic nature conservation is increasingly the norm, the picture is more worrying for heritage conservation. Monuments remain the legal property of descendants of the persons who erected them. In times of greater geographical stability, when families remained settled in one place, their tombs were carefully maintained with sums of money being left in wills to pay for their upkeep. Some tombs were painted, to keep them pristine, and regularly weeded. Seldom does this happen today; the culture of tending tombs has dwindled away. Some churchyards have suffered devastating clearances, and their interest is forever spoiled.

Why do tombs decay? Plants, particularly ivy, can throttle a monument, and cause it to collapse; such growth might look picturesque, but it can lead to trouble. As the plant establishes itself, water gets inside, which causes iron cramps to rust; the stone components can then split, dislodging the structure. More plants can then grow in the gaps, and eventually push the

The grand early Georgian memorial at Chipstead (Surrey) to the Rev. John Tattershall (d.1740). Water gets inside such structures, causing iron cramps to rust; the components of the tomb them start to fall apart. Regular maintenance can prevent plant growth which worsens the problem. This tomb has been repaired since the photograph was taken in 2012.

structure apart. Subsidence is another problem: the irregularity of below-ground conditions can cause brick vaults and foundations to tombs to subside, and sometimes topple over. Loose pieces such as urns then become vulnerable to theft or loss.

Stone is a natural material, and many headstones will steadily weather away: the pleasure to be had from them will not last forever. Moisture can get inside, weakening the stone's structure and drawing salts to the surface; the repeated cycles of saturation and drying out cause the once-strong material to weaken. Some sandstones are prone to lamination, when whole sheets of loosened stone fall off, carrying inscriptions away with them. Many headstones had quite shallow relief carving, which can easily erode and become hard to decipher. Yet another problem can be caused by railings: many chest tombs were once surrounded by these, and if left unattended they can rust and collapse.

In recent years, Health and Safety concerns have led to memorials (often Victorian or later ones, which were less securely made) being taken down: flaws in their construction have made them unstable. Levelling historic tombs is to be resisted unless absolutely necessary, but it is essential to take seriously any structural issues. Specialist advice is needed in such situations, and qualified conservators are brought in to advise. Graveyards are not playgrounds but they should not be no-go zones either.

Relentless decline is the lot of the majority of churchyard memorials. In some places, however, steps have been taken to prolong their life. In Painswick (Gloucestershire), often regarded as the country's finest churchyard, conservation steps began to be taken in 1973, when some perished masonry elements began to be re-carved, and a new technique of chemical preservatives started to be applied. The restoration has now weathered in, but the chemical

Right: At Painswick churchyard, an ongoing programme of re-carving perished elements of this outstanding group of monuments since the 1970s has maintained their meaning and dignity; carefully executed, such interventions will blend in and prolong the value of these tributes to the dead.

Above left and right: Before and after: the Grade II listed Hollis tomb in Beaconsfield (Buckinghamshire) had suffered from drastic settlement and was close to collapse. Cliveden Conservation Workshop rebuilt the monument, dating from *c.* 1785, for £13,000 in 2005.

solution turned out to be a mistake as it trapped moisture inside the stones, and actually hastened decay. Active involvement in conserving memorials prolongs their legibility and even their very existence: it also helps encourage the centuries-old crafts of stone-carving and masonry. Nowadays, conservators are well-versed in dismantling tombs and overhauling them, addressing subsidence and replacing rusting iron cramps with stainless steel ones. Subsidence can topple tombs, and careful reinstatement using experienced conservators can rescue memorials from collapse.

Did you know?

Painswick (Gloucestershire) has the highest number of individually listed monuments of any churchyard in England: over eighty are protected in this way. There are safeguards for all tombstones through churchyard regulations.

Caring for monuments can be complicated and expensive, but there is help at hand. The National Lottery Heritage Fund is committed to helping communities protect these special places, and Historic England has helped both by providing guidance (see What Next, below), and can help with fund-raising; specialist groups too can help parishes in raising awareness. Many parishes benefit from the work put in by devoted volunteers: this can range from keeping weeds at bay, to carrying out recording projects.

Keeping a survey of the churchyard memorials inside the church helps regular worshippers and visitors make connections with the parish dead who lie beneath their tombs: perhaps the growing popularity of family history can help connect more people with their ancestors, and contribute to the care of their irreplaceable memorials. Churchyard trails have great educational potential: they can connect modern audiences with present nature, past lives, and bring attention to geology and the craft skills of the past.

Remarkable gravestones from the heroic age of the railways: these two memorials at St John the Baptist, Bromsgrove (Worcestershire), commemorated two workers killed in an accident in 1840. Made of painted sandstone, they were restored in 2014; the Railway Heritage Trust paid for half of the costs.

7
What Next?

Further Reading

The best work on the subject is Frederick Burgess' *English Churchyard Memorials* (1963, reprinted in 1979 and 2004). The fruit of a lifetime of looking, it covers the historical and design aspects equally well. An early history of the subject is Mrs Stone's *God's Acre: or, Historical Notices relating to Churchyards* (1858). Hilary Lees' books include studies of Cotswold, Cornish and Wiltshire graveyards, as well as her survey volume, *English Churchyard Memorials* (2000). For Scotland, Betty Willsher and Doreen Hunter's *Stones: 18th Century Scottish Gravestones* (1978) is a fine survey of a rich tradition; Willsher's *Understanding Scottish Graveyards* (revised edition 2005) and Dane Love's *Scottish Kirkyards* (2010) provide further overviews.

Thomas W. Lacqueur's *The Work of the Dead. A Cultural History of Mortal Remains* (2015) is a sweeping study of attitudes to burial which places the churchyard in its international context, while Peter Jupp and Clare Gittings's *Death in England. An Illustrated History* (1999) sets the English scene. On medieval graveyards, Sally Badham's *Medieval Church and Churchyard Memorials* (2011) is the best starting point. Warwick Rodwell's *The Archaeology of Churches* (2012) explains the subterranean sensitivity of churchyards and their relationship with the church building. Julian Litten's *The English Way of Death: The Common Funeral Since 1450* (1992) provides the historical background to burial and mourning, while James Stevens Curl's *A Celebration of Death* (1980) sets out the rich cultural background of funereal design.

Nature is covered in Francesca Greenoak's *God's Acre: The Flowers and Animals of the Parish Churchyard* (1985). Stefan Buzcacki's *Earth to Earth. A Natural History of Churchyards* (2018) is a brisk survey which touches on management too. The *Churchyards Handbook*, now in its 4th edition (2001), published by the Church of England, gives much advice about sympathetic management. Harold Mytum's Recording and Analysing Graveyards (2000) is of help when surveying a churchyard, and for an archaeological take on the topic.

Useful Websites

Caring for God's Acre (www.caringforgodsacre.org.uk) is a very helpful site with much advice on offer on the natural aspects of churchyard conservation.

Historic England (https://historicengland.org.uk/) has several relevant publications on monument conservation and on the significance of burial grounds: practical advice is available at https://historicengland.org.uk/advice/caring-for-heritage/cemeteries-and-burial-grounds/monuments/. It also hosts the National Heritage List for England (https://historicengland.org.uk/listing/the-list/), the Government's statutory record of protected heritage assets, including churchyards. Historic England's Archive contains a rich collection of potentially relevant historic images to help with research: see https://historicengland.org.uk/images-books/photos/englands-places/.

For Scotland, a good starting place is the Archaeology Scotland website, with a section devoted to graveyards: https://archaeologyscotland.org.uk/projects/scottish-graveyards/

Each Church of England diocese will offer advice and guidance to those seeking to carry out any works within consecrated ground: the Church of England's ChurchCare website includes advice on churchyard structures: https://www.churchofengland.org/more/church-resources/churchcare/advice-and-guidance-church-buildings/churchyard-structures

A useful place to start if thinking about fund-raising is the Heritage Funding Directory (https://www.heritagefundingdirectoryuk.org).

The Mausolea and Monuments Trust is a charity dedicated to funerary architecture, with a clear conservation mission. Its website (www.mmtrust.org.uk/) includes a gazetteer of all known mausolea which is a useful place to start.

A good place to discover the modern revival in tombstones is the Lettering Arts Trust which can also put you in touch with appropriate artists (https://www.letteringartstrust.org.uk).

Getting Involved

Volunteers can help with the maintenance and upkeep of a churchyard: contact the incumbent and churchwardens to see how you can be of use. Making a record of the memorials in the churchyard, and researching the persons buried there through parish records can be an effective way of widening interest in local history. Carrying out a survey of the memorials, and keeping a digital record, can also help monitor their condition and identify which ones need attention. The ChurchCare website (given above) stresses the importance of using qualified conservators for any repairs: these would need prior approval, so do seek out advice from the vicar. Always take care exploring churchyards: trip hazards abound, and tombs can be unstable.